# Ada
## and
# Zaz

Written by Sally J. Pla

Illustrated by Rebecca Burgess

# Collins

# 1 Zaz Jones

Sebastian ("Zaz") Jones was a thoughtful, sensitive boy who lived with his nan and their parrot, Albertina, in a tiny one-room flat in a busy city.

It was a tight fit, living in their tiny flat. But they managed well enough. Zaz had his side of the room, Nan had her side, and Albertina had the spot by the window. Nan would work at her desk, while Zaz busied himself at his, writing in his blue notebooks.

He wrote plans for building robots, cars and ships. He drew maps of the neighbourhood, and of the bus route from home to school. He recorded information about the new dentist's office, to help him prepare for an upcoming visit.

Because Zaz was a person who very much liked to know what to expect.

Nan and Zaz loved their little parrot, Albertina.

"Albertina gave you your name, you know," Nan said to Zaz. "When you were two and first came to live with me, Albertina kept asking you, *What's your name? What's your name?* But you couldn't quite pronounce 'Sebastian', so she thought you'd said, 'Zaz'," said Nan, smiling.

"Hello, Zaz!" sang Albertina, as usual. She said it dozens and dozens of times, every day.

Zaz groaned.

"Hey!" said Nan, teasing. "Not many people have the privilege of being named by a bird!"

3

Zaz very much liked his orderly life with Nan. She always collected him from school at the exact right time. She took him to therapy, to help him improve his speech and coordination skills. She kept him supplied with blue notebooks. And she served his favourite meals just how he liked on his favourite plate, with none of the food items touching.

Zaz's five favourite meals:

Nan worked hard to take care of them both.

Zaz worked hard, too, at school. But the sounds, sights, movements and lights of the school day often wore him out. The buzz of bells in the halls felt like needles in his ears. The flicker of overhead lighting made his eyes ache and his head pound.

So, once he got home, he'd need to be quiet for a bit. He'd rest under his heavy orange blanket, which calmed his fidgety, tired body. He'd put on his noise-blocking headphones. And soon he felt much better.

Nan called it "Sensory Reset Time". She needed it, too, so she completely understood.

Albertina also seemed to understand. During Sensory Reset Time, she would only squawk very softly.

"Oh, Albertina. You're my best friend. But – "
Zaz paused. "I hope I'll meet a human best friend someday. Someone just like me."

"Hello, Zaz," said Albertina, her beady eye giving a knowing wink.

# 2 Ada Higgins

Across the city, in a small building on a leafy street, Ada
Higgins lived with her mum, dad and big dog, Marvel.

Ada was active and bold, impulsive and inventive!
Her hobbies included:

- baking creative concoctions

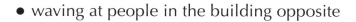

- tap dancing

- waving at people in the building opposite

- pulling pranks on Alan the postman

- playing the trumpet
  (well, the three notes she knew)

- taking Marvel on walks

- playing two kazoos at once

- and reciting the alphabet backwards
  (but not while playing kazoos).

Ada was a friendly, outgoing girl who liked EVERYONE she met! And most people liked her back. (Except Mr Brown in 4-D, who was grumpy.) But she had never quite managed to have the kind of friend who stuck with you. A through-thick-and-thin friend. Where you basically lived at each other's houses, laughed at the same jokes and overlooked each other's faults. A friend who wouldn't mind her mix-ups and mess-ups. Because sometimes, Ada had to admit that she did overdo things a bit.

She sat by the window with Marvel and looked out at the city. "Do you think I'll ever find that kind of friend, Marvel? A best friend?"

# 3 Nan's announcement

All morning, in the tiny flat, Nan had been strangely thoughtful and preoccupied. Now she was tapping her teaspoon on the rim of her cup, over and over.

Finally, Zaz couldn't take it anymore.

"Nan? Is something bothering you?" he asked.

Nan smiled and took a deep breath.

"Well, my goodness. I do admit I have something important to tell you, Zaz. It's good news, but it will mean a big change. The two of us will need to keep talking it over, until you feel comfortable."

Zaz got a dreadful flutter in his stomach. What could she be talking about?

Nan reached for his hand. "The news is … well, we're going to be moving!"

Zaz was stunned. "MOVING? But why?" he blurted.

Nan waved around at the cluttered space.

"Because you're getting bigger, and this place is just too small for us. Also, the new flat is much more convenient for my new job. And here's the best part: it's in a lovely building, and there's a bedroom for each of us! Oh, wait till you see it, Zaz!"

Zaz covered his ears and started rocking.

Nan came and hugged him around the shoulders. "We'll keep talking about it. I know change can be especially hard for you, Zaz. But this will be a *good* change. I promise!"

Zaz went under his blanket and hid.

How could Nan do this to him? Make him leave the only home he'd ever known? Sure, it was cramped, and they didn't have any privacy, or space, and it was far away from Nan's job. But … SO WHAT?

After a while, though, Zaz started to think more clearly.

It *did* make sense to be closer to Nan's work, and to have more space.

And he *did* trust Nan to make good decisions for them.

Zaz had to admit that moving felt like a logical decision.

The main thing worrying him, though, was *not knowing what to expect.*

He would feel anxious until he got his questions answered.

So, he grabbed a blue notebook.

"What's the new address? What floor will we live on? What's the neighbourhood like? When will it happen? What should I know in advance?" Zaz was full of urgency. "I need to know what to expect."

Nan smiled. "Let's get to work, then! We'll fill your notebook with everything you need to know."

After a few hours of work, a blank page of Zaz's notebook was transformed into this:

Mike's Movers

start packing    finish packing

| | 1 | 2 | 3 | 4 | 5 |
| 6 | 7 | 8 | 9 | 10 | 11 | 12 |
| 13 | 14 | 15 | 16 | 17 | 18 | 19 |
| 20 | 21 | 22 | 23 | 24 | 25 | 26 |
| 27 | 28 | 29 | 30 |

load van    moving day

4-B

new flat

FLOOR PLAN

The postman, Alan. Nan says he's friendly.

Zaz was still sad. But he was starting to feel flutters of hope and excitement, too.

They were ACTUALLY MOVING! It felt like the biggest thing that had ever happened to him. At least, that he could remember.

# 4 The Very Big Day

Ada Higgins was so beside herself with excitement that she couldn't sit still. Someone new was moving in across the hall today! Alan had told her all about it. He said it was a woman with a grandson – and he was about her age!

There had never been anyone her age in the building before! Not to mention, just across the hall!

She'd rushed to tell Mum and Dad.

"Why, that's fabulous!" they'd said. "We'll have to think of a nice way to welcome them."

Hmmm … Ada's thoughts had raced. Maybe a song on the kazoo? *BZZZZT!* Or, on *two* kazoos at once! Double-kazooing was one of her talents!

Maybe she could teach kazoo to the new boy! Then, they could make a wild joyful racket of noise together! Oh, she hope-hope-hoped he would like it here. They could have so much wild, noisy fun, pulling pranks and herding pigeons and things like that!

Ada did a happy-jig.

"Woof!" Marvel put his paws on her shoulders, and Ada danced him around the kitchen. "NEW BOY, NEW BOY, NEW BOY!" she sang.

"Awooo!" said Marvel, his back legs sliding in a puddle of milk.

"Ada, please! Think of the neighbours!" Mum called. "It's barely six o'clock in the morning!"

Dad appeared, yawning. When he saw the kitchen, his eyes shot wide open. "Ada Louise Higgins! What have you done?"

Ada looked around. Oops!

How had *that* happened? She couldn't remember making such a mess!

"I'll clean it up, Dad! I was baking a welcome cake for the new neighbours! They're moving in TODAY! TODAY, TODAY, TODAY!"

Suddenly, Ada smelt something.
Mum and Dad did too. They sniffed.
Marvel sniffed ...
*SMOKE!*

"Oh, Ada!" Dad rushed to take a charred pan out of the oven. "You KNOW the rules are never to cook without supervision!"

"I wasn't cooking," Ada said. "I was baking!"

Dad gave her a warning look.

"Well, the cake might be salvageable. But we need to talk about you trying harder to slowwww down, to stop and think and be aware!"

Ada had heard that before, but it was extremely hard for her to do! Ada's brain liked to happily rush ahead – that was just how she was.

"I'll work on it, Dad," Ada said. And she meant it.

"That's my girl! Now help me wash these dishes."

As she helped Dad, Ada got to thinking.

A half-burnt cake was not nearly a good-enough welcome for the new neighbours. She needed something better …

*Ping!* A fantastic idea popped into her head. Ada gasped, threw down her dish towel, and tore off down the hall. "I'll be right back! I need to ask Miss Lee something!"

"Ada! Please don't bother that poor woman this early!" called Mum.

But Ada wasn't listening. She was imagining the most amazing new-best-friend-across-the-hall Welcome Fanfare Extravaganza ever!

And Miss Lee in 4-C had what she needed to make it happen!

# 5 Moving

For Zaz, Moving Day seemed to arrive in no time at all.

Even with a detailed timeline to follow and a notebook full of things to expect, and even after many encouraging talks with Nan, Zaz still felt a cold knot of terror twisting inside him as the removal van pulled up.

"WAIT!" Zaz shouted. "The photos we found showed it's supposed to be a red removal van. It's blue!"

"But it's still a Mike's Movers van," said Nan gently. "Everything will be OK."

Zaz wasn't convinced. What if *more* things turned out to be wrong and unexpected about this move? What if *everything* did?

# 6 Miss Lee

Miss Lee in 4-C ran a dancing school, and her wardrobes and shelves held fabulous old costumes and showy props. Ada loved visiting her.

"Honestly, Ada Higgins," Miss Lee said, with a yawn. "Do you know how early it is?"

"I have a tap shoe emergency!" said Ada. "A new boy is moving into 4-B today, and I need to perform a Welcome Extravaganza!"

Miss Lee threw up her hands. "A welcome what? A tap shoe emergency?" She sighed. "Well then!" – and she went rummaging in her wardrobes.

# 7 En route

It felt funny to be on the motorway in Nan's old car, following behind a big removal van. It felt loose and strange and free, as if Zaz didn't quite belong anywhere anymore.

He gulped and clutched his blue notebook tightly to his chest.

"Soon, you won't need those notes," Nan said, glancing at him from the driver's seat. "Soon, you'll see your new home in person, *for real.*"

Zaz gulped again. He wasn't sure if that sounded thrilling, or terrifying.

# 8 Ada's welcome

*Tippity clackity clackity!* Ada was practising her tap dance.

"Woof!" said Marvel.

"Ada, please," said Mum, who was trying to work.

"I have it all planned out!" said Ada. "First, I'll play the double kazoo. Then I'll do a tap dance and sing a welcome song I made up. Then, trumpet." She scratched her head. "Do you think three trumpet blasts are enough?"

Dad looked up from his book. "I like your enthusiasm, Ada, but please make sure you're not disturbing them! Moving day is a busy time."

Just then, a whistle of van brakes floated up to their window. Ada rushed over and looked out.

She saw a little red car pull up in front of a removal van.

A boy got out and stared anxiously at the building.
In his arms, he clutched a blue notebook. The boy opened
the notebook, placed a finger to mark his page, then looked
down and up, down and up.

What was *that* all about? If Ada were him, she wouldn't
just stand there looking at a book! She'd run around and
start exploring!

"They're coming into the lobby!" Ada yelled.
She scooped up her cake, kazoos and trumpet and rushed
down the stairwell to greet them. Her tap shoes echoed
with a surprisingly satisfying *CLACKITY CLACKITY CLACK!*

By the time Ada got to the lobby, she was panting. The trumpet banged her ribs, the kazoos poked her through her pockets, and the cake kept sliding around on the plate.

"Where are they? Where are they?" she called out to Alan.

"Why, hello, Ada. Who, the new folks?" he said. "They just went up."

"GAH! Thanks, Alan!"

"The boy looked a bit green around the gills," he added.

"Just wait 'til he meets ME!" she said. "He'll feel better then!" She banged on the button for the lift.

# 9 Ding-dong!

Zaz Jones was entering Flat 4-B, his new home, for the first time. It was sunny, spacious and quiet. The wooden floors creaked pleasantly underfoot. And down a short hallway were two whole separate bedrooms! Zaz felt a flutter of excitement.

Nan set down Albertina's cage on top of a moving box and looked around happily. "So, what do you think?" she asked. "It's great, isn't it?"

Zaz smiled.

"You can choose which bedroom you – "

*Ding dong!* Just then the doorbell rang. Zaz jumped.

"Who could that be?" wondered Nan.

This was unexpected. Zaz couldn't handle a new person at the door right away! He wasn't ready. In a sudden shy panic, he looked around for a place to hide.

It was a girl around Zaz's age, with messy hair and a giant smile.

"I'm Ada," she said, panting loudly. "From across the hall!"

"How lovely to meet you!" Nan said. "I'm – "

Ada cut her off. She was too impatient to get started on her welcome. *TOOT TOOT!* went her trumpet.

Nan tried again. "How nice to – "

But Ada had picked up two kazoos. *BZZT BZZZT!*

Zaz, peeking out from the coat cupboard, covered his ears.

Now Ada was tap dancing. It sounded like firecrackers on the hallway tiles. *CLACKITY TAP!*

Then she started to sing:

"WELCOME, WELCOME, YOU'LL LOVE THE FOURTH FLOOR!

"I'M ADA HIGGINS! I'LL GIVE YOU A TOUR!

"WE HAVE LOTS OF FUN IN STORE!"

She pinwheeled her arms around and kicked out her legs in a grand finale: "Ha-CHA Ha-CHA!"

Nan was delighted. She clapped and laughed. "My goodness, Ada, how – "

But now, Ada had picked up a cake plate and held it out to Nan. "It tastes OK. We scraped off the burnt bits."

"Well, isn't this kind?!" said Nan.

Ada's eyes darted around. "Where's your grandson?"

"He was right here!" said Nan, turning. "Zaz?"

Zaz knew he should come out and say hi, and part of him longed to. But that meant revealing that he'd been hiding. *How embarrassing!* People didn't usually understand his shyness and his need, sometimes, to hide.

And so, he stayed silent as Nan made excuses and said goodbye.

# 10 Ada, disappointed

Ada slumped back across the hall and flung herself across the sofa. She tooted gloomy notes on the kazoo, then announced: "The new boy is NOT going to be my best friend."

"Oh dear," said Mum. "How so?"

Ada swiped angrily at a tear on her cheek. "He wouldn't even come out to say hi!"

Marvel came to rest his warm chin on her knee. Ada hugged him gratefully.

"Moving days are hard," Mum said softly. "Maybe he was still sad to be leaving his old life. Maybe he was struggling with a lot of feelings."

"Well, he sure made a bad first impression," Ada grumbled.

Mum was thoughtful. Then she asked, "Do you remember way back when we got Marvel? You yanked his tail, and he barked at you and made you cry. You said you hated him and wanted us to send him back."

Ada gave Marvel's nose a kiss. "I was wrong."

"Sometimes it's easy to get off on the wrong foot. I wonder if maybe this boy just needs a little bit of time to, well, warm up," said Mum.

"Hmmm … Like I needed time to warm up to Marvel."

The more Ada thought about Mum's words, the more sense they seemed to make.

Had she been a bit hasty?

I'm losing everything familiar!

Where's my stuff?

I'm saying goodbye to everyone I know.

More thoughts occurred to Ada.

Where had the boy moved from?

Why did he live with his grandmother?

What had he been looking at in that blue notebook?

What were his hobbies?

Would he go to her school?

How old was he?

She'd been so focused on her welcome, she forgot about them getting to know each other.

Maybe she needed a new approach.

Marvel had gone to get his red ball. He dropped it gently in front of Ada and looked up, wagging, pleading.

"Oh, Marvel," Ada said, throwing the ball for him. "*Everyone* loves *you. You* never have trouble making friends."

"Woof!" said Marvel, leaping to make a perfect catch.

"In fact, you're a friend magnet," Ada told him grumpily.

Then, suddenly, she sat up straight.

She had a new idea!

# 11 Zaz reconsiders

After Ada had left, Zaz emerged, sheepishly, from
the coat cupboard. He felt squirmy inside, and flushed
with embarrassment.

"I'm sorry, Nan. I just couldn't handle it."

Nan patted his shoulder. "It's OK. I do think that girl
was a little disappointed not to meet you," she said.
"But I understand. Don't worry. We'll get your room set up.
Then you'll feel better."

They got to work. They unpacked boxes, hung pictures,
made his bed and arranged his shelves.

Nan set his stack of blue notebooks on the desk.
"That should just about do it!"

Zaz looked around. How odd to have all the old and
new so jumbled up together! But Nan had been right.
He was going to love having his very own room!

"Happier now?" asked Nan.

Zaz nodded.

"Nan? I think I'm ready. I'd like to try again to say hi to the neighbour, Ada."

Nan smiled. "I think that's a great idea!"

"But what if she blows her trumpet again?"

"Then just ask her nicely to stop. Explain that you tend to be a sensory avoider – you don't like noises or bright lights or too much stimulation. She, on the other hand, is clearly more often a sensory seeker – she likes a lot of noise and action."

Zaz looked gloomy. "Maybe we're too different to be friends. Maybe we should stay far apart!"

"Could be. Or you might complement each other nicely! Never know until you try," Nan said.

Zaz thought about it. Then he had a clever idea: it was a lot easier to talk to people when Albertina was on his shoulder … What if he took her along, for support?

# 12 Trying again

At the same time that Zaz was planning to go and see Ada, Ada was planning to go and see Zaz.

"Come on, Marvel!" Ada called back into her flat. Now, where had he gone? She needed Marvel! He always made people smile. Now he'd help her break the ice with that shy new boy!

"Here, Marvel!"

She opened her front door, turned, and to her surprise, there in the hallway stood Zaz! And he had a bird on his shoulder!

"Whoa! Hello!" she said.

"Hello!"

Suddenly, Marvel came bounding out of Ada's flat. *Woof! Woof! Woof!*

"Eeek!" cried Zaz. He hadn't expected a dog.

And neither had Albertina. *Squawk!* Startled, she flew up to the top of Zaz's head. Then she flapped into the air.

"Marvel!" cried Ada. "DOWN!"

"Albertina!" cried Zaz. "Come back!"

Spooked by the dog, Albertina fluttered over to the stairwell.

Marvel lunged. *WOOF! WOOF! WOOF!*

"Stop! STOP! DOWN, Marvel!" Ada tried to catch his collar.

"HE'S GOING TO HURT MY BIRD!" Zaz shouted.

"HE WOULD NEVER!" Ada shouted back.

But the bird and the dog were already squawking and woofing down the stairwell.

Ada and Zaz flew down after them.

Ada's parents and Nan rushed into the hall.

"What on earth?" they asked each other.

Miss Lee in 4-C opened her door. "What is this calamitous racket?"

As for grumpy Mr Brown in 4-D, he was out of town, thank goodness.

Ada and Zaz stumbled out into the lobby. There was no sign of their animals, but poor Alan was on the floor!

"I slipped going after that bird," he said, groaning and sitting up. "I'm afraid the dog's got it now." Alan glanced toward the postboxes.

Zaz froze. His eyes bulged with horror. Cold, steely horror.

Sure enough, Marvel slunk forward … with something in his mouth.

"No. No!" shouted Zaz. It was too terrible! He couldn't unsee the horror: colourful feathers were visible, sticking out between Marvel's teeth.

But then Marvel did a remarkable thing. He came over to Zaz and spat Albertina out at his feet.

Zaz thought he might faint. How could his best friend be lying there, lifeless?

"Noooo!" shouted Ada from somewhere. "It can't be!"

"Wait!" said Nan. "Watch! Something's happening!
Do you see?"

Zaz couldn't believe his eyes.

Albertina suddenly started flapping … then she hopped
back upright!

She shook her ruffled feathers out as if to say, "What on
earth was THAT?!"

Everyone cheered. Nan looked Albertina over carefully. "She seems completely fine," she marvelled.

Ada's mum said, "Golden retrievers are bred to carefully retrieve birds. They have a deep instinct for handling them gently."

"That's right," said Alan. "They have what's called a 'soft mouth'."

"So Marvel didn't want to hurt Albertina," said Ada.

"Only to *retrieve* her," said Zaz, in awe.

# 13 Welcome party

Nan invited everyone up for cake.

The Higginses, Miss Lee and Alan chatted together, while Nan served up the slices and brewed the tea.

Mrs Higgins suddenly stopped chewing. "Ada! What did you put in this cake?"

Ada grinned. "Black pepper! Do you like it? I think I have a talent for creative baking!"

Some of the guests didn't look so sure.

Zaz showed Ada his new room.

"It's great! And tomorrow I can show you the park," said Ada. "You can help me herd pigeons." She thought for a moment. "We'll leave Marvel at home."

"Fine by me," said Zaz. "Then we can come back here to write up our pigeon observations in my notebooks."

"Fine by me," said Ada. "How's the pepper cake?"

Zaz took a small bite. As he chewed, he looked around at his new home. He listened to Nan and the guests laughing in the kitchen, and to Albertina, singing.

"Honestly? This isn't *too* bad," he said.

"I bet it's better than you expected!" said Ada.

The new friends looked at each other and laughed.

# Zaz's notebook

## Moving Day

Why a blue, not a red removal van?

talked a lot with Nan

me

Girl across hall!

Nicer than I expected!

tried again ...

Marvel chased — then saved Albertina!

Nan said Albertina is fine!

My new friend!

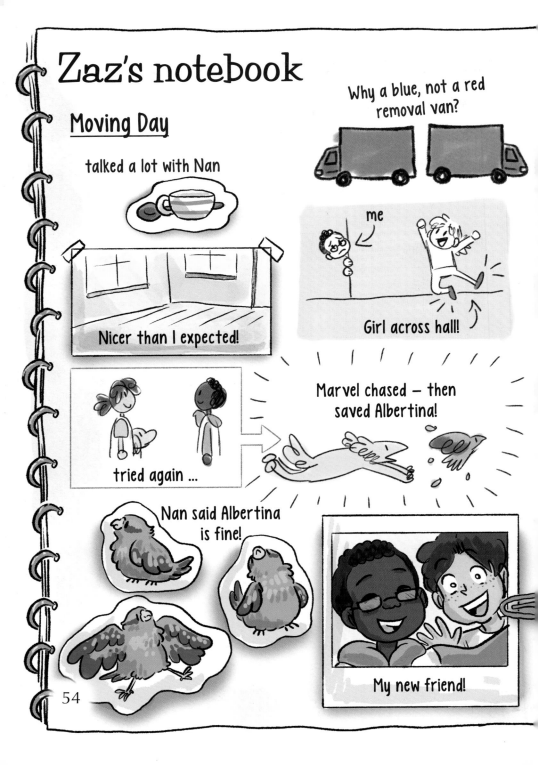

# Ada's notebook (a gift from Zaz!)

Welcome, welcome, you'll love

the fourth floor! I'm Ada Higgins!

I'll give you a tour! We have lots

of fun in store!

CAKE INGREDIENTS
butter, sugar, self-raising flour,
<u>lots</u> of black pepper!

NOTE TO SELF:
Learn about
parrots!

NOTE TO SELF:
Return Miss
Lee's tap shoes!

NOTE TO SELF:
Do not
return them
before noon!

NOTE TO SELF:
Finish cleaning
kitchen mess.

NOTE TO SELF:
Meet Zaz
in park!

Bring
this notebook!

Bring Kazoos!

# Ideas for reading

Written by Gill Matthews
*Primary Literacy Consultant*

**Reading objectives:**

- check that the book makes sense to them, discussing their understanding and exploring the meaning of words in context
- ask questions to improve their understanding
- draw inferences such as inferring characters' feelings, thoughts and motives from their actions, and justifying inferences with evidence
- predict what might happen from details stated and implied

**Spoken language objectives:**

- ask relevant questions to extend their understanding and knowledge
- use relevant strategies to build their vocabulary
- articulate and justify answers, arguments and opinions

**Curriculum links:** Relationships education – Caring friendships; Respectful relationships

**Interest words:** thoughtful, sensitive, orderly, therapy, coordination, fidgety

## Build a context for reading

- Give children time to explore the front cover. Discuss where they think the story takes place.
- Read the back-cover blurb. Ask children for their impressions of the two characters.
- Point out that this is a contemporary story. Explore children's knowledge and understanding of the text type.
- Ask what they think might happen in the story. Encourage them to support their responses with reasons and evidence from the text.